WALKING *with*
JESUS

Devotions for
Lent & Easter 2025

WALKING *with* JESUS

Devotions for Lent & Easter 2025

Editors of *Mornings with Jesus*

A GUIDEPOSTS DEVOTIONAL

A Gift from Guideposts

Thank you for your purchase! We want to express our gratitude for your support with a special gift just for you.

Dive into **Spirit Lifters**, a complimentary e-book that will fortify your faith, offering solace during challenging moments. Its 31 carefully selected scripture verses will soothe and uplift your soul.

Please use the QR code or go to **guideposts.org/ spiritlifters** to download.

Walking with Jesus: Devotions for Lent & Easter 2025

Editors of Guideposts

Published by Guideposts
100 Reserve Road, Suite E200
Danbury, CT 06810
Guideposts.org

Cover and interior design by Pamela Walker, W Design Studio
Cover photo by Adobe Stock
Typeset by Aptara, Inc.

ISBN 978-1-961251-89-2 (softcover)
ISBN 978-1-961251-90-8 (epub)

Printed and bound in the United States of America
10 9 8 7 6 5 4 3 2 1

"Lent is about becoming, doing, and changing whatever it is that is blocking the fullness of life in us right now. Lent is a summons to live anew."

SISTER JOAN CHITTISTER

O Love, How Deep, How Broad, How High

O love, how deep, how broad, how high,
how passing thought and fantasy,
that God, the Son of God, should take
our mortal form for mortals' sake!

He sent no angel to our race,
of higher or of lower place,
but wore the robe of human frame,
and He Himself to this world came.

For us baptized, for us He bore
His holy fast, and hungered sore;
for us temptations sharp He knew,
for us the tempter overthrew.

For us to wicked men betrayed,
scourged, mocked, in crown of thorns arrayed,
He bore the shameful cross and death
for us at length gave up His breath.

For us He rose from death again,
for us He went on high to reign,
for us He sent His Spirit here
to guide, to strengthen, and to cheer.

All glory to our Lord and God
for love so deep, so high, so broad—
the Trinity whom we adore
forever and forevermore.

—Attributed to Thomas à Kempis

Introduction

Why does Lent exist? It exists because faith cannot flourish in a bubble, like a flower under glass. Our faith needs to be lived, stretched, and tested. Lent gives us the opportunity to pick up the faith we've been taught and carry it on our hearts, to emulate in our own small way the life and sacrifice of Jesus Christ, on the way to Easter's spiritual rebirth.

Bringing together some of Guideposts' most beloved writers and adding a few newer ones, *Walking with Jesus: Devotions for Lent & Easter 2025* offers observations and reflections on the season. Each heartfelt devotion is based on everyday life and experiences, reminding us that the season of Lent brings an unparalleled chance to walk alongside our Redeemer to Easter's glory. Paired with scripture and faith steps, these devotions invite us to stretch, strengthen, and, perhaps, test our own faith.

Lent isn't mentioned in the Bible, but its practice derives from Jesus's long withdrawal from society after being "led by the Spirit" (Matthew 4:1, NIV). God didn't cut off His Son from food and company for 40 days for no purpose. Jesus's stay in the wilderness was meant to test and strengthen Him. While in the wilderness, Jesus refuses every temptation Satan suggests, remaining stalwart in His devotion to God and His Word. Only after Jesus withstands these tests does He rejoin society, ready to begin His Gospel mission.

Jesus would never be far removed from suffering, as the tempests of Holy Week show. But, again, there was purpose for this. The book of Hebrews tells us, "[Jesus] had to be made like them, fully human in every way, in order that he might become a merciful and faithful high priest in service to God, and that he might make atonement for the sins of the people. Because he himself suffered when he was tempted, he is able to help those who are being tempted" (Hebrews 2:17–18, NIV).

Suffering, of course, wasn't exclusive to Jesus. Among the earliest Christians, even those who hadn't met Jesus before His crucifixion, were firm in their belief that great rewards would come after their worldly tribulations. As the Apostle Paul wrote:

"We also glory in our sufferings, because we know that suffering produces perseverance; perseverance, character; and character, hope."

—ROMANS 5:3–4 (NIV)

Suffering in this sense is both a character builder and a faith builder. "However, if you suffer as a Christian, do not be ashamed, but praise God that you bear that name" (1 Peter 4:16, NIV). Our difficulties today will make us better Christians tomorrow. And we are hopeful that better days—in heaven, if not here—await us. Indeed, what is Easter's jubilation but a glimpse of the paradise to come.

Pastor Timothy Keller wrote: "While other worldviews lead us to sit in the midst of life's joys, foreseeing the coming sorrows, Christianity empowers its people to sit in the midst of this world's sorrows, tasting the coming joy."

In keeping with the bright blooms of spring (Lent is an Old English word for "spring"), the Lenten season wears the vivid colors of a world bursting into flower after winter's dormancy. Like the natural beauty around us, we are invited to grow into better followers of the Lord over the 40 days. (Remember that our Lenten intentions and restrictions are relaxed on Sundays, which are dedicated for celebrating the Resurrection.) Paramount is our commitment to those practices that our God has taught from the beginning:

Pray. For Jesus, praying is an embodiment of His unity with His Father. Christ instructs us how to pray and even uses prayer to drive out evil spirits. His prayers are active appeals that extend even beyond the death He foresees for Himself. Regarding His disciples, he says, "My prayer is not for them alone. I pray also for those who will believe in me through their message, that all of them may be one, Father, just as you are in me and I am in you. May they also be in us so that the world may believe that you have sent me"

(John 17:20–21, NIV). By praying to the Father, we follow in the virtuous steps of Christ.

Fast. For Jesus, fasting has great purification power, as demonstrated by His time in the wilderness. He even advises us on its practice, making it a private affair, saying, "Your Father, who sees what is done in secret, will reward you" (Matthew 6:18, NIV).

Give. Among His Beatitudes, Jesus says, "Give to the one who asks you, and do not turn away from the one who wants to borrow from you" (Matthew 5:42, NIV). How better to model ourselves after the Savior who sacrificed His earthly life for our eternal one?

Lent is much more than a mandate against the little pleasures that give temporary happiness. More important are the opportunities it gives us to shoulder our small share of the Lord's burdens and sacrifices. Through our embrace of His examples of praying, fasting, and giving—by choosing the hard path over the easy road—we demonstrate our love of God and stretch our faith into His Grace.

Lisa Guernsey

ASH WEDNESDAY
MARCH 5

For everything God created is good, and nothing is to be rejected if it is received with thanksgiving.

1 TIMOTHY 4:4 (NIV)

LATELY, I'VE BEEN DOWNHEARTED, PLAGUED by negative thinking. My work wasn't going well, and I was discouraged. I couldn't even muster the enthusiasm to spend my regular devotional time with Jesus. But today I had a reason to cheer up. Whatacatch was back! My favorite item at Whataburger is the fish sandwich. But several years ago, the fast-food restaurant took Whatacatch off the menu except during Lent. But today was Ash Wednesday, the beginning of Lent. My daughter Brooke and I headed to lunch.

"If I play my cards right, I can have forty fish sandwiches," I said.

"Aren't you supposed to *give up* something for Lent?" Brooke asked. I would have answered but my mouth was full. Life was good again!

After I finished my sandwich, a nudge from Jesus got me wondering. Why wasn't I this happy every day of my life—grateful for waking up each morning with the gift of another day? Why did it take a sandwich to make me appreciate the life Jesus had given me? Then and there, I decided what I would give up for Lent—negativity and ungratefulness! And I would *give* thanks to the One who made this great gift of life possible.

I asked Jesus to forgive me for skimping on our time together and promised I'd do better. And I'd make it a habit to express my gratitude the moment I opened my eyes. Who knew a fish sandwich could be such a good teacher?

PAT BUTLER DYSON

FAITH STEP

As soon as you awaken each morning, thank Jesus for your life. Then pursue a day worthy of His gift.

THURSDAY
MARCH 6

Let Your mercy, O Lord, be upon us,
just as we hope in You.

PSALM 33:22 (NKJV)

AFTER MY DIVORCE, MY BIGGEST worry was my
children—how they would be affected. They had been,
and still are, the most important aspect of my life. Loving,
protecting, and guiding them—and teaching them about
Jesus—were and still are my focus. Mothering is my greatest calling. The coming apart of our family was something I
never wanted, and I felt deep shame about it. I had so much
guilt for allowing this difficulty into their lives.

The divorce was final in winter. As springtime came and
Easter approached, I desperately looked for signs of life. I
wanted to believe Jesus was going to do a new thing. I hoped
it would spring up any moment (Isaiah 43:19), but what I
mostly felt was tired. Empty. Sad and lonely. It was strange
doing all the usual activities and planning for the holiday
on my own, without my husband. Easter morning, I was

overjoyed to have my kids with me, but there was palpable weirdness to our celebration.

Jesus's resurrection from the dead took on new meaning for me that year. In many ways, my old self had died and was buried. I was forced to let go of the illusion that I had control over my life, my kids, and even the rate at which we all would heal. I threw myself on His mercy and waited, like a seed in the ground, hoping and trusting Jesus would raise me up and cause me to bloom in His time.

GWEN FORD FAULKENBERRY

FAITH STEP

Start some indoor seeds or buy bulbs to force.
Watch, wait, and trust sprouts to shoot up as you
pray for Jesus to raise up hope inside of you.

FRIDAY
MARCH 7

*God made Christ, who never sinned, to be
the offering for our sin, so that we could be
made right with God through Christ.*

2 CORINTHIANS 5:21 (NLT)

I COULDN'T WAIT TO TRY THE same-day home delivery benefit of my discount store membership. But I felt disappointed when my first order was dropped off. The store had made a few substitutions. The eggs were not extra-large, the pizza sauce was not our favorite brand, and the canned tomatoes were a different size from what I needed for a recipe. This feature did not turn out to be so convenient and timesaving after all.

Substitution isn't always a bad thing; it can be necessary, which is a major theme throughout the Bible. God designed the system of sacrifices and offerings laid out in the first seven chapters of Leviticus to atone for the Israelites' sins. This foreshadowed the day He would send the perfect Lamb, who would carry the sins of the world to the cross.

Jesus lived a sinless life, but He willingly offered Himself as a substitution for our punishment. Only the sacrifice of the sinless Christ was enough to bring forgiveness for our sins. Every bit of the horrific sorrow, abuse, pain, and suffering that Jesus endured paid for my sin. And for yours. I'm not sure I can ever comprehend such love.

Some days I'm tempted to substitute other activities for time I should spend with Jesus. But I find contentment and purpose only when I give Jesus first place in my heart. Nothing, and no one, can ever replace Him.

DIANNE NEAL MATTHEWS

FAITH STEP

Have you been trying to substitute something in the place Jesus should have in your life? Talk to Him about that.

SATURDAY
MARCH 8

Whoever is kind to the poor lends to the LORD, and he will reward them for what they have done.

PROVERBS 19:17 (NIV)

LAST SUNDAY AFTER ATTENDING CHURCH my husband, Michael, and I grabbed a quick lunch at Taco Bell before running a couple of errands. Walking out of the restroom after eating, I saw a young man in his late twenties make his way toward the exit. He held a Taco Bell sack in one hand and pulled a red carry-on bag with a duffel attached to the top, with the other. But what really caught my eye was the way the man looked at Michael. With piercing eyes, he whispered "Thank you" before walking out the door.

I was puzzled. Michael explained the man's card was denied when he tried to pay. "But he had a nice attitude about it and wasn't belligerent or angry, like some folks I've seen when this happens," Michael said, as he shrugged. "So I gave him cash to pay for his food."

I smiled. There have been several instances where Michael has done something like this during our 33-year marriage, a sneaky little act of kindness. I'm usually so preoccupied with my to-do list or where I'm going next that I may not notice people in need or their problems.

I've read many biblical accounts of how Jesus showed compassion to people in need: the outcasts, blind and sick people, and poor people. Reminded by Michael's charitable gesture, I pray that I, too, will grow in the gifts of showing Christlike compassion and mercy.

JENNIFER ANNE F. MESSING

FAITH STEP

Look for opportunities to do acts of kindness for friends, coworkers, family members, strangers, or anyone Jesus places in your path this Lenten season.

SUNDAY
MARCH 9

Don't embarrass me by not showing up;
I've given you plenty of notice.

PSALM 31:17 (MSG)

I WENT TO TEACH AT THE community center, but no one showed up. *They stood me up!* The next day, one of the students called, asking if I'd be there tomorrow. I said I'd been there yesterday, but no one showed up. She responded that they'd *all* shown up and waited for *me.* Then it dawned on me. Two of my clocks in the house and my clock in the car hadn't been changed to daylight savings time. And the clock at the community center was also an hour behind. It turns out, I was the one who didn't show up!

The next week, my mentor/coach in the UK didn't show up for our weekly online appointment. The following week, same thing again. Stood up *twice*—two weeks in a row, I messaged him to say I was waiting for our appointment. He asked if we'd changed our clocks or something. It turns out, they don't change *their* clocks until three weeks *after* the US. I'd been showing up to our appointment an hour early.

Jesus, why such confusion? Why can't we all be on the same time? And stay on the same time? Interrupting my grumbling, Jesus pointed out that He always shows up for me. No matter what time it is, day or night, Jesus is always on time. He reminded me of how He showed up for me at Calvary. By contrast, my struggle with time changes suddenly seemed insignificant.

CASSANDRA TIERSMA

FAITH STEP

While contending with daylight savings time changes during Lent, thank Jesus for His perfect timing in showing up for you at the cross. Also, double-check your clocks!

MONDAY
MARCH 10

How much more, then, will the blood of Christ, who through the eternal Spirit offered himself unblemished to God, cleanse our consciences from acts that lead to death, so that we may serve the living God!

HEBREWS 9:14 (NIV)

MANY CHRISTIAN TRADITIONS OBSERVE LENT, a somber time commemorating Jesus's 40 days in the desert before embarking on His earthly ministry. People are often encouraged to fast as Jesus did. Though I attend a church that doesn't observe Lent, I sometimes follow the tradition, attending mass on Ash Wednesday and giving something up. This year, I didn't. I fasted from fasting.

But I have fasted over the years. Last year, I fasted extensively as I sought God intently, wanting to hear His voice clearly. First, I fasted during my church's January fast. Next, I fasted during a challenging spiritual experience, wanting very much to understand what Jesus was showing me.

Finally, I worked on a demanding project and fasted as a way to receive divine inspiration.

Honestly, my fasts weren't very fruitful. In fact, something seemed way off.

I asked Jesus about it and listened for His reply. I realized He'd been urging me for some time to assume a posture of rest as a means of receiving His love. A type A doer who tends to brutal self-criticism, I hadn't been open to accepting Jesus's gentle invitation. That is why fasting had become empty for me.

I promptly and gratefully repented. Instead of fasting this Lenten season, I'm spending more quiet time with Jesus and simply enjoying life. It's sometimes uncomfortable for me to do nothing and be still, but Jesus is showing me that fasting from fasting can be joyfully freeing and faith-building.

ISABELLA CAMPOLATTARO

FAITH STEP

Whether you fast or fast from fasting, do it joyfully this Lent. Remember, you serve the living God–Jesus!

TUESDAY
MARCH 11

Then a cloud appeared and covered them,
and a voice came from the cloud:
"This is my Son, whom I love. Listen to him!"

MARK 9:7 (NIV)

I'VE ALWAYS BEEN FASCINATED BY the story of Jesus taking three of his disciples up high on a mountain, where they saw Him transfigured. But the part that dumbfounds me occurs when, on the way back down the mountain, Jesus tells them to tell no one about what they had seen—at least not until the Son of Man has risen from the dead (Mark 9:9).

I don't know how good you are at keeping secrets, but if I had just witnessed something that newsworthy, I'm not sure I could keep my mouth shut. I'm afraid I'd have been a total disappointment when it came to the whole "tell no one" order. I imagine that I would have justified it in my mind. *Was it really a request? He didn't mean not to tell my best friend, did He?*

I expect His disciples felt overwhelmed by having to keep quiet about what they witnessed. But they kept in mind that the voice in the cloud had told them to listen to Jesus. Holding on to this secret would have required patience and willpower that I doubt I could have maintained.

The disciples grasped the true significance of their directive. Jesus's words held meaning because of His trust in them. And they, through their faith in Jesus, did not disappoint Him.

JEANNIE HUGHES

FAITH STEP

The next time someone shares something and asks you not to tell anyone, practice what Jesus's disciples did. Tell no one.

WEDNESDAY
MARCH 12

*As he was praying, the appearance of
his face changed, and his clothes became
as bright as a flash of lightning.*

LUKE 9:29 (NIV)

WE RECEIVED A VISIT FROM a police officer this afternoon. I was pretty sure I hadn't committed a crime but was surprised nonetheless when I opened the door and learned why the officer was standing there.

He was holding back a smirk when he said he had a random question: Had I seen a peacock in the area? As a matter of fact, I had.

Henry, as my daughter dubbed him (the peacock, not the officer), had loitered in our yard several times over the past two weeks. Brilliantly colored in teals and purples, the feathery renegade was hard to miss against the backdrop of woods at the back of our property. He was not shy either, coming close to peek in the windows of our sunroom on his path from yard to yard.

Henry can't help but show his brightness. He simply lives as Jesus created Him. And it shows.

The peacock encounters left me thinking in a fresh way about the radiant effect of spending time with Jesus and what His love looks like on me. Is my time with Him beautifying my character? Is He hard to miss when others encounter me?

I hope Henry is more securely penned wherever he lives, but his presence brought my family unexpected delight. More important, sightings of my feathered friend prompted me to seek the beauty of my Savior's presence this Easter season.

ERIN KEELEY MARSHALL

FAITH STEP

Ask Jesus for eyes to see the radiance of His hard-to-miss presence. Then expect Him to reveal Himself to you. Leave it to Him to decide how and when.

THURSDAY
MARCH 13

Fixing our eyes on Jesus, the pioneer and perfecter of faith. For the joy set before him he endured the cross, scorning its shame, and sat down at the right hand of the throne of God.

HEBREWS 12:2 (NIV)

İT WAS THE WORST PAIN of my life. I was pretty certain that childbirth didn't hold a candle to the Crucifixion, however, as I made my way through transition, I would have been willing to openly debate that. Bringing new life into this world meant enduring intense, excruciating, agonizing pain. Yet I chose to do it not once but twice! Why? Because on the other side of that pain was joy. Those two tiny human beings brought me joy unspeakable!

My baptism into motherhood enabled me to better understand what drove Jesus to volunteer for the pain He went through as He endured the horrific brutality of the cross. He must have had His eyes on the other side of the suffering. His gaze was steadfastly fixed on the joy set before

Him. Jesus's vision was larger than the excruciating pain. He understood His suffering on the cross was a necessary step for us. His children. Those of us who would eventually become God's sons and daughters (Matthew 16:21–24).

That truth can get blurred and muddied by the world, our feelings, and evil. But I don't question it when it comes to my own children though. Every minute of labor and suffering was absolutely worth it to have them in our family. Likewise, Jesus joyfully suffered to make the way for us to become part of His family, forever.

KRISTEN WEST

FAITH STEP

Pull out baby pictures of children or yourself and feel unspeakable joy. Then meditate on a cross or crucifix and imagine Jesus's sacrifice and pain, knowing He joyfully did it for you.

FRIDAY
MARCH 14

Then Jesus was led by the Spirit into the wilderness to be tempted by the devil.

MATTHEW 4:1 (NIV)

T HE SPIRIT LED JESUS INTO the wilderness, a place devoid of beauty, where He would be tempted by the devil. But one by one, Jesus overcame every temptation offered. He returned from the wild fully aware of the battles believers wage against sins of all kinds.

This morning, I awoke in the midst of a personal wilderness. I'd experienced a dream steeped in sadness. Sorrow bled into my mood, souring the day. My mind was crowded with things I should have done but didn't, and items I wanted but couldn't have—a dark mix of regret and desire. In brokenness and desperation, I prayed.

Jesus's power flooded in, overwhelming the desolation of my soul, and reminding me I have all I need in Him. Every sin I've ever committed—even "that one"—is washed clean. I am never alone, even when challenged by temptations.

Jesus is with me today as I struggle with melancholy and shame. He was there for me yesterday as I fought anger. And He will be present for me, and for all of us always, in every trial and triumph, until the end of this age (Matthew 28:20).

Temptations can be difficult to bear. But they provide opportunities for our faith to be strengthened. We gain wisdom from the challenges. And like Jesus, we can emerge from times of trial as victors.

HEIDI GAUL

FAITH STEP

What temptations visit you in the wilderness of your soul? Write the sins that plague you on a sheet of paper. Pray for the wisdom to understand that testing can build spiritual muscles. Then write "victor" boldly across the sins you listed as you trust Jesus to tend to your needs.

SATURDAY
MARCH 15

May kindness and peace be yours from Jesus Christ, the faithful witness. Jesus was the first to conquer death, and he is the ruler of all earthly kings. Christ loves us, and by his blood he set us free from our sins.

REVELATION 1:5 (CEV)

*T*HESE ARE PERFECT, I THOUGHT, as I chose a bouquet of bright red tulips the week before Lent. I needed them for a sermon I would preach the following Sunday about the woman bent double in Luke 13. I figured by Sunday, at least one of the tulips would resemble a person bent in half.

After I filled a vase with water and placed it on the dining table, I remembered that putting a penny in the bottom of the vase causes the tulips to stand up straight. It worked! Those orangey-red flowers acted as if they'd won a spelling bee. I could almost see smiles on their faces. As it turned out, I needed smiles this week.

On Tuesday, we had to take my beloved cat Fred to be euthanized. He'd scratched our daughter too near her eye, and I couldn't take a chance that he might scratch someone else and cause permanent damage. I knew I was making the right decision. But I still grieved.

Yet every time I walked past our table during that dark, long week, those straight red tulips grinned at me. They reminded me of life everlasting, flowing from the blood of Jesus. My life from His death.

I thought my idea to buy tulips was for a sermon. Jesus knew I'd need them as a reminder of His precious love.

JEANETTE LEVELLIE

FAITH STEP

Buy some red flowers or place something bright red
in a prominent place to remind you of Jesus's sacrifice.
Every time you see it, thank Jesus.

SUNDAY
MARCH 16

Then shall the dust return to the earth as it was: and the spirit shall return unto God who gave it.

ECCLESIASTES 12:7 (KJV)

O N THE FINAL NIGHT OF our mother's life, my sister recorded everything Mom said. Mom would speak only a word or two, maybe a sentence, interspaced with long silences while her body continued to shut down.

"Green," she said.

"Do you see green, Mom?"

"Yes."

It was mid-February in the Northwoods. We knew the green she glimpsed was not of this world.

Among the final words of Jesus is a declaration that thrills me. "Into thy hands I commend my spirit" (Luke 23:46, KJV). In my Lenten heart-preparations, I've lingered over those words. As wise King Solomon said, eventually all human bodies return to dust, and the spirit returns to the God who gave it. Jesus didn't wait for death to instigate that process. He declared that at that moment that He was casting aside the human body He'd inhabited for 33 years and entrusting His spirit to His Father. Despite the enormity of the weight of the sins of the world crushing Him, Jesus's spirit was anchored to, in the care of, and returning to be reunited with the Father to whom He directly spoke.

Some scholars believe God the Father completely and utterly abandoned His Son when Jesus embodied our sins—became sin for us (2 Corinthians 5:21). I will forever be grateful that as Jesus gave up His spirit, He knew He had the ear of His Father when He said, "Into thy hands."

CYNTHIA RUCHTI

FAITH STEP

Which of Jesus's final words before His death hold your attention? Consider journaling your thoughts of why they matter so much to you. Then share the story with someone.

MONDAY
MARCH 17

A clean heart create for me, God;
renew within me a steadfast spirit.

PSALM 51:12 (NABRE)

I LOVE CRAFTING. WHEN MY DAUGHTERS Cassidy and Ana were little, I always had crafts ready. Showing them a sample beforehand, I would get right in there with them, my hands as glue- and glitter-covered as theirs. I paired each craft with a Bible story and verse for the children to remember, extending the learning. Teens now, the girls and I bake homemade bread together during Holy Week. Crafting cinnamon raisin, honey lemon and banana nut breads, we lovingly knead flour, water, and yeast together. With our dough-covered hands, we pour some into loaf pans. Others we shape into knotted rolls. With each one we bake, we share stories praying for the recipients of our gifts. Eventually, glorious smells fill our kitchen. It is a legacy I hope they share with their children someday.

Jesus was a maker too. He spent His life sharing stories to instruct us. From creation to the cross, He shows me the perfect example to follow. Teaching me how to fast (Matthew 6:16–18), pray and forgive (Matthew 6:9–15), and love (Luke 10:27). Jesus uses His holy Word and steady hand to mold me into becoming the person He wants me to be. Looking to Jesus and the Bible is the best recipe on how to create a beautiful and holy life, not only for myself, but for my children. And I can't imagine a better legacy to pass on.

GLORIA JOYCE

FAITH STEP

Whether it be with knitting needles or baking ingredients, seeds or craft paper, invite Jesus to join you in creating something for someone today.

TUESDAY
MARCH 18

Jesus answered, "It is written: 'Man shall not live on bread alone, but on every word that comes from the mouth of God.'"

MATTHEW 4:4 (NIV)

NO MATTER WHAT DAY OF the workweek it is, if I'm fasting, a box full of donuts or bagels appears in the office. As I feel myself instantly going into a doughy trance, I hear a voice in my head rationalizing why I can break the fast before I've even started it. In that situation, it's so tempting to give in and justify reasons to eat now and fast later.

Fasting is also tough for me, because I do not have a quiet cooperative stomach when it is empty. If I miss a meal, my stomach begins to growl—loudly, without any regard for where I am or who I'm with. It is especially vocal in church services and small meetings when my surroundings are quiet, whether a prayer, a sermon, or a pregnant pause in conversation. The simple thought of feeling embarrassed by this involuntary rumbling is sometimes enough for me to want to abandon a fast.

Fasting will always be a challenge when I focus solely on the natural effects of missing a meal. But when I focus on the spiritual benefits of fasting, such as gaining power to resist temptations and hearing the instructions of Jesus more clearly, fasting quickly becomes a necessity. Keeping a spiritual perspective motivates me to ignore unexpected treats and follow through with my intended fast. If only Jesus would do something about the unruly growling of my stomach!

ERICKA LOYNES

FAITH STEP

Read Matthew 4:1–11 before your next fast.
Ask Jesus to help you resist temptations of
all shapes, sizes, and flavors.

WEDNESDAY
MARCH 19

Near the cross of Jesus stood his mother...

JOHN 19:25 (NIV)

MY DAUGHTER, JOCELYN, TRIED OUT for the volleyball team at her middle school. The competition was fierce and, unfortunately, she didn't make the team. In an instant, her heart broke in two. I sat on her bed with her and witnessed her range of feelings go from anger to confusion to anguish. As she went through her gamut of emotions, I went through mine. In my anger, I drafted the email in my head that I'd send to the coach. In my compassion, I tried to come up with the right words to comfort Jocelyn. Yet no matter what I said or thought of doing, none of it consoled her. That's when I realized she needed me just to be there with her in the midst of her pain.

As Mary stood at the foot of the cross, I can only imagine what she was feeling and thinking. Was there someone she could beg or plead with to reverse the verdict and save her

Son? Were there words she could say that would console Jesus as He hung on the cross about to die?

Where I'm impulsive and a doer, Mary seemed to be intuitive and reflective. During Jesus's life, she'd pondered things in her heart, making her insightful and wise (Luke 2:19). Perhaps she knew the best way to show her love and support for her Son wasn't to be distracted by trying to fix the situation. Instead, Mary focused on being there, fully present, no matter how much it hurt, accompanying Jesus in the midst of His pain.

CLAIRE McGARRY

FAITH STEP

The next time someone is going through a tough time, just be present and accompany them in their pain.

THURSDAY
MARCH 20

Therefore we were buried with Him through baptism into death, that just as Christ was raised from the dead by the glory of the Father, even so we also should walk in newness of life.

ROMANS 6:4 (NKJV)

I'M NOT USUALLY A HAT-WEARER, but I thought it would be fun to buy matching Easter hats for my five-year-old granddaughter and me. I searched and searched and finally found two beautiful bonnets. Made of soft straw and stitched with glittery silver threads, the rounded tops and wavy brims were adorned with cream ribbons and flowers of turquoise, lavender, and pink.

When Sadie visited the next day, I positioned her hat on her head, giving it a slight downward tilt on the left side. I adjusted mine the same way and led her to a mirror mounted on the wall. As we admired our stylish spring attire, an old song came to mind, one my mom sang for me as a child: "In your Easter bonnet with all the frills upon it, you'll be the grandest lady in the Easter parade."

Decorative bonnets portray the newness of life in spring. Jesus nudges nature—shiny green leaves appear on trees, blossoms open on bushes and flowers, chirping birds criss-cross the sunny skies. Believers proclaim the resurrection of Jesus. And because God raised Jesus from the dead, we also celebrate our own promise of resurrection and eternity in heaven.

So put on your Easter bonnet, give it a bit of a tilt, and sing a song of praise to the Redeemer, the Lord of the Springtime. He makes everything new.

BECKY ALEXANDER

FAITH STEP

Put on a spring hat and breathe in some fresh spring air while you ponder what it means to "walk in newness of life."

FRIDAY
MARCH 21

He said to them, "How foolish you are, and how slow to believe all that the prophets have spoken! Did not the Messiah have to suffer these things and then enter his glory?"

LUKE 24:25–26 (NIV)

I'M READING THROUGH MY BIBLE slowly. Rather than race to the end to gain an overarching understanding, I turtle through scriptures, reading only until the Spirit gives me pause.

Sometimes, I make it through several verses to ponder throughout the day. Other times, a single word stops me. Today the word is *have*. When the risen Jesus is talking with two men on the road to Emmaus, individuals who couldn't believe what they were hearing about a man who had come to life again after crucifixion, Jesus said, "Did not the Messiah *have* to suffer these things?"

Why didn't the disciples understand the prophecies about Jesus's path to glory? That Jesus *had* to endure the torture, scorn, ridicule, betrayal, pain, all of it. That there was no other way than the cross.

Their doubts, their denial, their fickleness, their selfishness, their misunderstanding of God's promises and Jesus's purposes, their hope for a knight in shining armor who destroyed rather than an eternal king who brought life surely contributed to their blindness. It's why Jesus *had* to take our sins upon Himself. If even those closest to Him would not believe without His death and resurrection, would we?

As I approach Easter from a post-Easter perspective thousands of years later, I'm believing backward—moved by what Jesus said after He rose again to help me understand that there was no other way than the cross.

CYNTHIA RUCHTI

FAITH STEP

Write "no other way" on a strip of paper and drape it around a cross to remind you why Jesus had to die.

SATURDAY
MARCH 22

*There is a time for everything, and a season
for every activity under the heavens…a time
to search and a time to give up, a time
to keep and a time to throw away.*

ECCLESIASTES 3:1, 6 (NIV)

RECENTLY, I RECEIVED AN EMAIL informing me that my online computer storage was nearly full. If I didn't clear space, new files and photos wouldn't be saved. This minor inconvenience could become a big problem if I avoided making necessary changes.

So I spent time clearing out clutter. I deleted duplicate photos and videos and outdated files. It was refreshing to release what was no longer necessary or purposeful.

This season of Lent, I'm feeling led to get rid of clutter in my heart and mind too. When I take inventory of my inner life, I find emotional overload that needs to go, such as caring too much what people think, fear that Jesus will allow someone I love to suffer, and a pattern of low trust that He will bring truth to light and justice in situations I cannot control.

More vital to my well-being than a well-functioning computer system are a heart and mind freed up to fully engage with Jesus, others, and even with myself in healthy ways. By letting go of habits, patterns, or conveniences I rely too much on, I can focus more wholly on Jesus to meet my deepest needs.

So I keep clicking, enjoying the understanding that a healthy discard will keep me functioning without becoming overfull of what does not serve a healthy purpose.

ERIN KEELEY MARSHALL

FAITH STEP

Carve out 15 minutes for cleanup of a space in your life, whether it's a computer, a room, or a vehicle. Ask Jesus to reveal any area in your heart that needs decluttering.

SUNDAY
MARCH 23

And when the disciples saw Him walking on the sea, they were troubled, saying, "It is a ghost!" And they cried out for fear.

MATTHEW 14:26 (NKJV)

WHAT COULD BE WORSE THAN being tossed about at sea during a raging storm? Sailing the waves during a gale and spotting a ghost making its way toward you! Whenever I read this verse, I'm struck by the terror the disciples must have felt. Trapped and helpless, they must have felt that things were moving quickly from bad to worse.

In their fear, the disciples thought they'd seen a ghost. Instead, it had been Jesus coming to join them during their frightening journey. His presence calmed them, and the sea's churning waves died down.

I recently experienced my own "ghost" during one of life's storms. Over a little more than 3 weeks, I was involved in two auto collisions, neither of which was my fault. Between learning about multiple deductibles, car rentals, and other insurance details, I watched as the situation became financially scarier. One day when the claims adjuster called, my stomach dropped. I'd become so used to calamity that I'd come to expect it. But my fear was misplaced. She'd called to give me good news.

Like the disciples, the only time I panicked was when I questioned Jesus's presence in my situation. But Jesus was there during both accidents and their aftermaths. He's always present during the dark and dangerous journeys of life. And as long as I keep my focus on Him, I can remain calm.

HEIDI GAUL

FAITH STEP

What "ghosts" are camouflaging Jesus's place in your mind?
Make a list of your fears and let Jesus guide you
through the storm. Trust Him to take care of you.

MONDAY
MARCH 24

But God demonstrates his own love for us in this:
While we were still sinners, Christ died for us.

ROMANS 5:8 (NIV)

I STOOD IN OUR APARTMENT IN Uganda the morning before
we flew home. Aromas of bacon and fried potatoes lingered in the air. Four other ladies and I had traveled there to
meet the children and encourage the staff of three mission
schools we supported.

Our week at the schools had rocketed by with lively
worship services under jackfruit trees, tours of the campuses,
and my favorite, getting to know the children. Many of
them were AIDS or war orphans with nowhere else to go.
The schools were their only hope. Everyone we met thanked
us for coming to visit.

Our kitchen helper, Peace, and I were alone on this last
day. As she thanked me for the one-hundredth time, I asked,
"Why is it so important to you that we visit here? Wouldn't

it be a better use of the money I spent on this trip if I sent you a check?"

Peace took my face in her slender and soft hands and gazed into my eyes. "Mama Jen, anyone can send money. You loved us enough to come. You can't put a price tag on love." Tears pooled in my eyes. All I could manage was a nod and a hug.

Of course, I thought of Jesus.

Jesus wasn't content simply to send help. He came in human form to show us what God was really like. To heal, forgive, and save. To change our very nature. To make us daughters and sons of God (Galatians 4:4–7).

And the price He paid was Himself.

JEANETTE LEVELLIE

FAITH STEP

Show Jesus you love Him by doing something out-of-the-ordinary and in person for someone in need.

TUESDAY
MARCH 25

For God so loved the world that He gave His only begotten Son, that whoever believes in Him should not perish but have everlasting life.

JOHN 3:16 (NKJV)

"JEFF GOT HIS HEART!" My cousin Sandra's exciting news was an answer to countless prayers. Sandra's brother, Jeff, had been on the transplant list for months, after a massive heart attack had irreparably damaged his heart. A husband, father, and grandfather in his early sixties, Jeff was gregarious, generous, and athletic. He still had lots of living to do. And now he could! *Thank you, Jesus.* When I asked about the donor, all Sandra knew was that he had been a 22-year-old man from southwestern Louisiana, who had lost his life in a construction accident.

The next day, a story in my local Beaumont, Texas, newspaper caught my eye. A 22-year-old southwestern Louisiana man named Matt had died in a construction accident. *Jeff's donor?* Puzzled that Louisiana news was reported in our

Texas paper, I passed along the information to Teri, Jeff's wife. Although organ donor families and organ recipients don't meet unless both parties agree to it, Teri felt an unmistakable prompting from Jesus to attend Matt's funeral anonymously. Sitting on the back row of the church, she paid tribute to Matt and to his parents for their unfathomable gift.

Later, Jeff and Teri were able to meet Matt's parents, and they became friends. For almost 17 years, Jeff lived a full, joyous life because of Matt's heart. Several weeks before Easter, when Jeff went to heaven, Teri said, "Now Jeff will be able to thank Matt in person." A fulfillment of the promise of Easter.

PAT BUTLER DYSON

FAITH STEP

Thank God for His Son Jesus, whose sacrifice assures us we will see our loved ones again.

WEDNESDAY
MARCH 26

Jesus said to them, "Come and have breakfast."
None of the disciples dared ask him,
"Who are you?" They knew it was the Lord.

JOHN 21:12 (NIV)

I LOVE WORKING IN VOCATIONAL MINISTRY. Part of my role includes caring for those on our church staff team. One of the ways I do this is to sit down periodically with them over coffee or a meal. I've lost count of how many times, during these very informal visits, Jesus shows up. Hearts are opened and trust is fostered. Sometimes the answer to prayer is revealed and clarity for the person's next step, in life or ministry, is embraced.

Jesus modeled simple relational moments like these following His death and resurrection. John 21 provides an incredible account of Jesus inviting some of His disciples to breakfast on the beach following a divinely orchestrated catch of large fish. I can almost imagine the waves lapping onto the shore and hear their casual, yet meaningful, conversations around the crackling fire.

Jesus's death and resurrection made a way for everyone to have an individual relationship with God (John 3:16). Because of this magnificent work of love, we are invited to sit down and enjoy daily bread with Him. We have personalized access to talk boldly with Jesus about our cares, worries, fears, and concerns.

As I celebrate this deeply meaningful season, I plan to periodically sit in the presence of Jesus and listen carefully to Him.

KRISTEN WEST

FAITH STEP

Over coffee or a meal, pull up an extra chair and wait for Jesus to show up. Listen to what He has to say.

THURSDAY
MARCH 27

This took place to fulfill what was spoken through the prophet: "Say to Daughter Zion, 'See, your king comes to you, gentle and riding on a donkey, and on a colt, the foal of a donkey.'"

MATTHEW 21:4–5 (NIV)

SCROLLING THROUGH SOCIAL MEDIA, IT struck me how many iterations of Jesus are represented by various groups in our culture. Some of the loudest describe Him as a political hero who conquers whoever they oppose. Perhaps the greatest contrast I observed was an image of a big, burly Jesus flexing his muscles, and in another post, Michelangelo's *La Pietà*. This famous rendition imagines a thin, marble Jesus lying dead across his mother's lap. The kaleidoscope of online options caused me to consider who Jesus is to me.

A multifaceted God-man (John 10:30) emerges from the New Testament accounts. He raised the dead (Mark 5:21–43), fed multitudes (John 6:5–14), healed the lame (John 5:1–16). He rebuked demons (Luke 4:35) and turned over tables in the temple in righteous anger (Matthew 21:12–13). He suffered and died on the cross and appeared to women and His disciples as the resurrected Lord (John 19–20). And in Revelation 19:11, Jesus is seen in a vision as a rider on a white horse who comes back for His people.

Still, it's the King who rides into Jerusalem on a donkey who speaks to the deepest part of me this Lenten season. The One who eschews power and riches offers what we all really need: a gentle Savior.

GWEN FORD FAULKENBERRY

FAITH STEP

Think about who Jesus is for you. Draw a word cloud describing Jesus and hang it where you'll see it often.

FRIDAY
MARCH 28

My comfort in my suffering is this:
Your promise preserves my life.

PSALM 119:50 (NIV)

OUR FAMILY, LIKE MANY OTHERS, prepares for Christmas by setting up a Nativity scene. When our children were young, I wanted a way to help them prepare for Easter. I didn't want to move mindlessly through the season. I hoped that Jesus's sacrifice would sink into their minds. I didn't believe I could discuss the Resurrection with my children without starting at the beginning—the joy of Jesus's birth, followed by His trial, suffering, and death. So I dug around in the Christmas decorations and pulled out the crèche once Lent began.

Next, we hard-boiled a dozen white eggs and poured vinegar into cups. The kids stirred in color pellets of blue, yellow, and red. They sat at the kitchen table, in threadbare aprons. Taking their time, they painted the eggs with cotton swabs to mimic the Christmas characters. The shades seemed to bring the eggs to life as they recreated the Nativity scene using Easter eggs instead of figurines.

After the eggs dried, we assembled our Easter Nativity using the Christmas crèche. Remembering how Jesus was wrapped in swaddling clothes, they wrapped their Baby Jesus egg in gauze. Then I read them the Easter story from their children's Bible.

That Lenten season, my children were in awe and had many thought-provoking questions about Easter and Jesus—*egg-xactly* what I hoped!

JEANNIE HUGHES

FAITH STEP

Instead of just coloring Easter eggs, consider creating an Easter Nativity. When you read about Jesus's resurrection, don't forget to read about His birth.

SATURDAY
MARCH 29

See, your king comes to you, righteous and victorious, lowly and riding on a donkey.

ZECHARIAH 9:9 (NIV)

WHEN MY KIDS AND I drove past a converted carriage house the other day, the front door was open, and a man in a tuxedo and white gloves stood at the entrance. Additionally, the walkway up to the door was lined with a red carpet and velvet theater ropes on both sides. We tried to imagine what elegant event was happening, lamenting we weren't invited. Days later, I learned the carriage house was for sale. What we'd seen was an open house the Realtor decorated to attract more buyers. Turns out we could have gone after all, since it was a public showing.

That spectacle made me curious about where the red-carpet tradition came from. I discovered it's believed to have originated in the ancient Greek play *Agamemnon*, written in 458 BC. When Agamemnon returns from the battle of Troy, his wife lines the walkway from his carriage to their door in crimson silk. Even though only the gods were deemed worthy of such luxury, she thought a conquering lord's feet shouldn't touch the dusty ground.

My conquering Lord Jesus deserved the red-carpet treatment too. As people saw Jesus entering Jerusalem on a donkey, they knew someone extraordinary was in their midst: someone so important, neither His feet, nor His donkey's hooves, should touch the dusty ground. So they laid down their cloaks and palm fronds, lining His path as a way to pay homage to the Only One who is worthy of such royal treatment.

CLAIRE McGARRY

FAITH STEP

What red-carpet treatment can you show to others this Lent that will serve to line Jesus's path in homage to Him?

SUNDAY
MARCH 30

Jesus has the power of God, by which he has given us everything we need to live and to serve God. We have these things because we know him.

2 PETER 1:3 (NCV)

I'M GIVING UP SLEEP FOR Lent. This wasn't intentional. It just happened. I'd been considering the idea of giving up something for Jesus during Lent. But my carnal nature overpowered my good intentions. My appetite for food won out. The only tangible thing I've given up is carbonated water, which will be a permanent arrangement. Then, accidentally, I found myself giving up sleep. Was this healthy? Or safe?

Knowing Jesus is my sufficiency (2 Corinthians 12:9), I trust it'll be His power, not mine, that'll get me through… even when I'm sleep-deprived. While singing and worshiping late into the wee morning hours before Sunday morning music rehearsal, I know Jesus will give me everything I need to live and to serve God. The strength and endurance to make it through music rehearsal and the Sunday morning song set, even when I haven't had enough sleep.

Jesus always comes through. Today, He graciously provided an extra window of time for afternoon rest on the Lord's Day. I'm so grateful for the truth in these words of Paul: *My God will richly fill your every need in a glorious way through Christ Jesus* (Philippians 4:19, GW). Even when it's just the energy needed after giving up sleep for Lent.

CASSANDRA TIERSMA

FAITH STEP

Is your energy flagging during this Lenten season? Embroider or use a Sharpie to write the words of 2 Peter 1:3 on the hem of a pillowcase. Let it remind you of Jesus's power when you can't sleep.

MONDAY
MARCH 31

And walk in the way of love, just as Christ loved us and gave himself up for us as a fragrant offering and sacrifice to God.

EPHESIANS 5:2 (NIV)

M Y SON ISAAC'S BIRTHDAY FALLS in April, usually right around Easter. Isaac has Down syndrome so up until he turned 14, an egg hunt was a big part of the birthday fun. I've always invited a mix of kids to Isaac's parties, including his special classmates, typical peers, siblings of attendees, big brother, Pierce, and his crew, all athletes. The egg hunts risked being totally inequitable, but for my pre-hunt coaching to Pierce and his friends.

Of course, those jocks could swarm the egg hunt, grabbing all the eggs in a flash. They could out-hunt Isaac and his buddies, who tend to move more slowly and ponder their acquisitions more carefully, sometimes totally overlooking the brightly colored eggs.

Thus, I'd convene a discrete meeting beforehand, reminding the competitive older boys to hang back, coach the stragglers, and ensure the guest of honor and his posse got a good haul.

Sometimes, the big boys had to walk alongside some of the kids, stand in front of the eggs and coax them to bend over and reach down until the egg was securely in their basket. It was a sweet sight to behold—the only slightly older boys sacrificing their fun and loot to enhance the experience for the others.

When I remember those Easter egg parties, it's hard not to think of Jesus's lifegiving sacrifice for each one of God's children…including you and me. Thank You, Lord.

ISABELLA CAMPOLATTARO

FAITH STEP

On strips of paper, write down ways you can enhance the Easter experience for others. Put those ideas in plastic eggs, randomly placed around your house. Open them often and take action.

TUESDAY
APRIL 1

Christ is the head of the church, his body,
of which he is the Savior.

EPHESIANS 5:23 (NIV)

I RECENTLY SPOKE AT THE UNIVERSITY where I graduated from the honors college three decades earlier. For the Founder's Day celebration, I was asked to present stories about the founder, who was my mentor, and the early days as he and others established his vision for the honors college. Current students walked to the microphone and shared their experiences; then the director tied it all together, connecting the founder's vision to the current program.

On my way home, I thought about how proud I believe my mentor would be if he saw the honors college today. It made me happy to go back there and see his vision being carried out by people faithful to it, who share the same mission even though he is gone.

I wonder how Jesus feels when he looks at the church today—those of us who call ourselves Christians and participate in defining what modern Christianity looks like—not only how we present ourselves in culture but also our church rituals. The ways we practice and preach. How changed the vision of the Founder and His mission seems to be, to me. Perhaps Lent and Easter are the perfect opportunity to pause and reflect—our own Founder's Day celebration.

GWEN FORD FAULKENBERRY

FAITH STEP

Write a speech as if you were asked to describe Jesus, as the founder of Christianity, to someone who doesn't know Him. Consider how you carry out His vision as your Mentor.

WEDNESDAY
APRIL 2

He who did not spare his own Son, but gave him up for us all—how will he not also, along with him, graciously give us all things?

ROMANS 8:32 (NIV)

I'VE BEEN THROUGH ENOUGH SEASONS in my life to understand that I don't always get what I want. A first marriage that ended in divorce, a child that went prodigal, and a journalism career that never came to fruition, just to name a few. I wish I could say that I victoriously soared through those seasons of heartache and disappointment, but that was not the case. I would love to testify that I hung on tight to Jesus every step of the way and firmly believed that He was enough to get me through it all, but I didn't. My daily walk looked very similar to the Dow Jones Industrial Average graph in a shaky financial climate as I doubted, then believed; believed and then doubted again. Up, down, down, up, deep dive down. But Jesus, who is ever so patient, held on tight to me and helped me eventually learn a very simple and foundational truth: Jesus + Nothing = Everything.

No matter what trials I may encounter or how challenging my circumstances may be, Jesus is sufficient. Jesus is my everything. If all else were to be stripped away and I only had Jesus, I would still have everything. Isn't that at the heart of why we celebrate Easter? Our Savior's victory over the grave gives us this great confidence. All that we will ever need is Him. Because He is everything.

KRISTEN WEST

FAITH STEP

Label what you are waiting for on a graph with highs and lows. Shade the entire page with a highlighter, representing Jesus. Keep it as a reminder that He is your everything.

THURSDAY
APRIL 3

*How lovely is your dwelling place, L*ORD
*Almighty! My soul yearns, even faints, for the
courts of the L*ORD*; my heart and my flesh
cry out for the living God.*

PSALM 84:1–2 (NIV)

WHEN I READ BIBLICAL DESCRIPTIONS about the Lord's
home, I can't even begin to imagine how splendid
and lovely it is. The psalmist longed to be in God's courts
because he was refreshed by the Lord's presence and the
majestic essences of His dwelling place. I've walked through
the gorgeous Butchart Gardens in Canada, and the dazzling,
five-star Manila Hotel in the Philippines. From such experiences, I know that beautiful surroundings rejuvenate and
inspire me. Magnificent spaces have a way of making me
intimately aware of Jesus's abiding presence.

This is why I've always endeavored to keep our house as
lovely as I can. I know a well-maintained, cozy home can
minister to my family, bringing peace and refreshment to

their hearts. A home does not need expensive, designer furnishings to be beautiful. Careful thought can add warm, decorative touches to every room. Keeping it clean is a blessing to me and my family. I strive for cheerful, welcoming surroundings to create a sacred refuge in a cold world that sometimes brings discouragement.

I believe everyone needs a peaceful, comfortable space to seek Jesus's presence. Whether praying or resting, a well-kept home gives me physical as well as spiritual rejuvenation.

JENNIFER ANNE F. MESSING

FAITH STEP

Think about how you can better seek Jesus and soak in His comforting, loving presence. Do two things to beautify your home this Lenten season.

FRIDAY
APRIL 4

I thank my God every time I remember you.

PHILIPPIANS 1:3 (NIV)

FOLLOWING A WINTER OF DISAPPOINTMENT and sadness, I was weary. The loss of my father-in-law and my husband's layoff weighed heavy. I couldn't seem to rally for another season of sacrifice as Lent approached. Surely, I could find some way to honor Jesus for his gift on the cross. But, lost in my own darkness, nothing came to mind. Sitting down at my desk, my eyes fell upon the pile of unopened notecards I'd purchased a few weeks before. I'd planned to reach out and thank those who helped my family over the past several months. Jen, who brought delicious meals even with a colicky infant at home. Sarah, who encouraged me with her prayers amid her own family's strife. Kris and Mike, who drove two-plus-hours in traffic and brought food for the post-funeral luncheon. So many others who offered support to my family. So many to thank. If only this were Thanksgiving.

Grabbing a pen and a notecard, I began writing. As words of gratitude poured onto the page, I felt lighter, more energetic. Writing thank-you notes lifted my spirit and helped me remember that I had also gained blessings during this season of loss.

Praying for each person as I wrote their card, I hosted my own personal Thanksgiving at Eastertime, sending my love and appreciation across the miles. Gratitude—what better way to honor Jesus during Lent for His sacrifice?

GLORIA JOYCE

FAITH STEP

Think of someone you know who could use a kind word. Send a short note or text today to thank them for their friendship.

SATURDAY
APRIL 5

But your iniquities have separated you from
your God; your sins have hidden his face
from you, so that he will not hear.

ISAIAH 59:2 (NIV)

MY SON WAS TALKING TO me from another room the other day. He had the door shut so I couldn't hear a word he was saying. All I could decipher was *wah-wah-wah*, like the adult's dialogue in Charlie Brown cartoons. I went to the door, knocked and waited for him to let me in. Once he did, I had him repeat what he'd said, and we talked about it.

This experience made me think about how my bad choices construct walls around my heart, metaphorically, putting me in a room away from Jesus. When I stand strong in those bad choices, I put a door on that room and close it. Of course, Jesus is always standing outside my door, waiting to be asked in (Revelation 3:20). Repentance opens the closed door of my heart. It allows me to hear Jesus and to relate to Him.

There's no better time to repent than Lent. It's a time when I specifically reflect on all that Jesus did for me on the cross. Keeping the door of my heart open to Jesus, I realize His blood sacrificed for us is the key that provides redemption and forgiveness (Ephesians 1:7) for you and for me.

CLAIRE McGARRY

FAITH STEP

Find a key around your house. Use a sharpie to write Jesus on it. Put the key on a ribbon and wear it around your neck or place it somewhere prominent to remind you that Jesus's sacrifice unlocked the door.

SUNDAY
APRIL 6

*We tell you the good news: What God promised
our ancestors he has fulfilled for us, their
children, by raising up Jesus.*

ACTS 13:32–33 (NIV)

TO HELP A FRIEND AVOID conflict during a challenging
child custody situation, I offered to pick up her son
from his dad during the week of Easter. I rang the doorbell
and waited, my stomach doing somersaults. When the door
opened, there stood little Jesse clutching a teddy bear and his
6-foot dad holding a suitcase.

"I have good news!" I exclaimed.

"What?" Jesse's dad asked.

I stretched out my arms and took it up a notch. "The
Savior is risen!"

"Uh, uh, yes, He is," Jesse's dad stammered. He leaned
down. "That's the truth, isn't it, Jesse?"

My dramatic declaration, I must say, surprised all three of
us. I'm not sure what came over me or where it originated

but it worked. Any tension that existed before the door opened disappeared in an instant. Jesse gave his dad a good-bye hug and skipped beside me all the way to my car.

I should interject the good news of the Resurrection more often. When things get difficult in my own house…when a stranger is rude to me at the grocery store…when I'm exhausted from working long hours…when the TV tells me the world is falling apart. I can spread my arms and testify to the victory of Jesus over death and the grave. I might receive a few raised eyebrows from the people around me, but that's OK. Jesus is alive, and saying it aloud is the best stress reliever ever.

BECKY ALEXANDER

FAITH STEP

Stretch out your arms and catch someone off guard today by proclaiming: "I have good news! The Savior is risen!"

MONDAY
APRIL 7

When Jesus tasted the vinegar, he said, "It is finished." Then he bowed his head and died.

JOHN 19:30 (NCV)

MY GRANDDAUGHTERS WERE EXCITED THAT I had promised to knit them scarves from the yarn of their choosing. But as the time grew near for my next visit, I hadn't finished the second one. I knew between the long drive and the first couple of days at their house, it would get done. I started to put Lilah's scarf in a pretty gift bag with tissue paper, but decided against it since I couldn't do that with Leo's. How would Leo have felt pulling out an almost finished scarf still on the wooden needles, attached to a ball of yarn and with loose ends hanging off? I had more work to do.

With His last words from the cross, Jesus declared that His mission was finished. As the perfect Lamb of God, Jesus offered Himself as the once-and-for-all sacrifice for sin. I have no need to try to earn my salvation by following a set of strict rules or laws. No need to rack up enough good deed points before I come to Him. In fact, nothing I do or don't do can add to or take away from Jesus's work on the cross. I need only believe and accept His forgiveness and unconditional love.

I often get bothered when I see projects I've half-finished, or even bought supplies for but have yet to begin. But I am always grateful that my Savior left no loose ends hanging with His work.

DIANNE NEAL MATTHEWS

FAITH STEP

Are you stressed out over projects or chores you haven't completed? Let that feeling remind you of what Jesus finished out of love for you.

TUESDAY
APRIL 8

Let your roots grow down into him, and let your lives be built on him. Then your faith will grow strong in the truth you were taught, and you will overflow with thankfulness.

COLOSSIANS 2:7 (NLT)

I LOVE TO GO ON WALKS through my entire neighborhood. It's a 45-minute trek, and spring is one of my favorite times for it because of the explosion of white blooms on the pear trees that line the streets. It's a gorgeous display in the middle of Lent.

There are a few downsides, however. Those lovely blooms have a short season, and they're surprisingly stinky, like slightly rotten eggs. Then there's the issue of pear trees' shallow roots. They are notorious for lacking sturdiness, and the trees are frequent casualties of bad storms.

Lent is a season for deepening our focus on Jesus's sacrifice, and the pear trees remind me of a few truths to take deeper into my heart. I want roots that grow more sturdy in Jesus each year, and I want my life, words, actions, and thoughts to beautifully reflect His character and love. It's also my desire that those qualities last long and don't fade after a fleeting season. So this year during Lent, I'm asking Jesus to keep growing me in those ways, because they don't happen naturally without His help.

I'm keeping in mind the lessons of the pear trees, and I am grateful for how He reveals Himself in the nature He created.

ERIN KEELEY MARSHALL

FAITH STEP

Write a prayer of thanks to Jesus for the unique ways He reminds you to go deeper with Him during Lent. Thank Him for some aspect of creation that reveals His character or reminds you of His love for you.

WEDNESDAY
APRIL 9

Forget the former things. Do not dwell on the past.

ISAIAH 43:18 (NIV)

MY HUSBAND, JEFF, ENJOYS BRINGING me shirts from conferences he attends. My heart sank when I saw the color of his latest gift. "I can't wear turquoise," I said. Jeff wanted to know why, so I related the sad saga of the turquoise Easter dress.

As a girl, buying a new Easter dress was something I looked forward to all year. My family couldn't afford many new clothes, so I chose the dress carefully. Mom and I went to the Smart Shop, and after trying on multiple dresses, I selected a beautiful turquoise shirtwaist. When I got home, I tried it on again. I paused from twirling in front of the mirror and was horrified! In daylight, the vibrant turquoise drained my fair complexion to a pasty white, with ghastly undertones of yellow.

"Mom," I wailed, "I can't wear this. Let's take it back!" But Mom said it was too late, so I wore the dreadful dress. In the decades since, no turquoise garment has come near me.

"Wow," Jeff said, "you're good at holding on to things. Like that grudge against Cathy." *Ouch.* Sometime back, Cathy's and my young sons had gotten into an altercation, and we all had exchanged angry words. The boys had gotten over it, but Cathy and I hadn't. I'd prayed about reconnecting with Cathy, and I knew Jesus expected me to do so, but my pride wouldn't let me make the first move. *Do it!* I felt Jesus whisper. *Yes!* I silently answered. And maybe I'd bring her a cute turquoise shirt.

PAT BUTLER DYSON

FAITH STEP

Make a list of three things you are holding on to from the past. Let them go!

THURSDAY
APRIL 10

Jesus wept.

JOHN 11:35 (NIV)

I SAT AND CRIED WITH A friend, who'd lost her sister after an extended illness. Her grief was palpable, and my heart went out to her. On the way home, my thoughts turned to the time Jesus showed a glimpse of His humanity. He too cried with friends after they told Him Lazarus was dead. I can comprehend only a tiny fragment of the deep sorrow Jesus experienced at the loss of His dear friend, as He shared in the agony that Lazarus's sisters Mary and Martha suffered.

I believe the emotions Jesus faced were more complex than mourning—infinitely more heartbreaking because He is God. He knew that but for the introduction of sin into our world, death wouldn't exist at all (Genesis 3). Jesus was fully aware of what awaited Him in the future. Pain, humiliation—even death, for a time—would be required of Him. Lazarus was but one in need of a new life. All of us would require Jesus's action for restoration and eternal life.

Had mankind not sinned, death would never have existed, nor would we need Him to fight the battle on the cross.

Today when I wept for my friend, I also wept for the suffering I caused Jesus. I believe that when Jesus wept for Lazarus, He wept for me, for you, for every one of us. For what we could have been and for what we are. And I hope He shed a few tears of joy for what we will someday be, in Him.

HEIDI GAUL

FAITH STEP

Be present for a friend who is mourning by visiting or making a phone call. Remind her that you and Jesus are grieving alongside her.

FRIDAY
APRIL 11

*If a man has a hundred sheep, and one
wanders away and is lost, what will he do?
Won't he leave the ninety-nine others and go out
into the hills to search for the lost one? And if
he finds it, he will rejoice over it more than
over the ninety-nine others safe at home!*

MATTHEW 18:12–13 (TLB)

"HAVE YOU SEEN MY BEST watch, honey?" I asked my husband several weeks ago. Although I sometimes misplace items, I'm careful about the expensive watch my former boss gave me. I'd recently noticed the clasp had slipped open once or twice and made a mental note to have it repaired. But my mental notebook had failed me.

Kevin and I looked in the dish where I put my watches at night. We looked on top of the microwave in the church kitchen, where I place my watch when I wash dishes after a potluck. I even called my doctor to see if the watch had fallen on her floor.

My watch is still missing. I cringe at the thought of losing that valuable piece of jewelry.

I also cringe when I remember the times I've run away from Jesus—either by refusing to do what I know is right or by hiding from Him when I think He's let me down.

Jesus never lets me stay lost. Like the Good Shepherd He is, Jesus searches for me until He finds me hiding behind a boulder of regret or pouting beneath a heap of disappointment. Sadly, my watch is still lost. But thankfully, Jesus never gives up seeking, searching, and calling my name until He finds me.

JEANETTE LEVELLIE

FAITH STEP

Are you hiding from Jesus? Close your eyes and picture yourself letting Him find you as you run to Him.

SATURDAY
APRIL 12

But a time is coming and is already here when the true worshipers will worship the Father in spirit [from the heart, the inner self] and in truth; for the Father seeks such people to be His worshipers.

JOHN 4:23 (AMP)

Typically, on an Easter Sunday, I'm in Memphis attending church and celebrating Jesus's Resurrection with my husband and son. However, last Easter I was in Chicago. I'd flown there a couple of days earlier to help my sister, who had been caring for our mother. Mom had fallen and broken her ankle in three places five weeks ago. She was still recovering from her injuries, so I took vacation time to visit her, and to give my sister a short respite.

For long time Christians like Mom and me, our Easter Sunday didn't look or feel very Easter-y. Neither of us dressed up, went to church, or ate a holiday-themed meal that day. Instead, I spent the day helping my mom get around on her walker, making a food prep plan, and giving thanks to God for her healing. I couldn't help feeling a little let down without a significant Easter celebration.

While I experienced quite an unconventional Easter, I was reminded that Jesus was the ultimate disrupter of traditions and expectations. He confronted the legalistic actions of religious people and concentrated on the internal activity of one's heart (Luke 13:10–17). In the same way, what I was doing last Easter was much more significant than where I was.

ERICKA LOYNES

FAITH STEP

Are you faced with the possibility of an unconventional Easter Sunday? Evaluate your circumstances and determine how you can still celebrate Jesus's Resurrection without traditional activities.

PALM SUNDAY
APRIL 13

They took palm branches and went out to meet him, shouting, "Hosanna! Blessed is he who comes in the name of the Lord! Blessed is the king of Israel!"

JOHN 12:13 (NIV)

A N UNAPOLOGETIC NERD, I COULDN'T help but be enthralled to study the palm branch's rich and revealing symbolic history. Like many things in scripture, understanding the cultural context and individual elements makes the power of His-story come alive. Jesus's passionate arrival into Jerusalem is loaded with ancient meaning, starting with the palm.

All these historical insights seem to foreshadow Jesus and His ministry in vivid ways. Assyrian religions considered palms a sacred tree. For the ancient Egyptians, palm stems represented a long life. In ancient Greek mythology, palm leaves were the symbol of Nike, the winged goddess of victory, and Greeks awarded winning Olympic athletes palms. The Romans soon broadened the palm's celebratory use to honor any kind of victory—in athletics, in court, or in battle.

Jesus's palms heralded eternal life and victory over sin and death.

Celebrating Jesus with palms can be seen as the eternal fulfillment of these mortal gestures. Jesus's triumphal entry on that first Palm Sunday heralded the promise of eternal life, the One True God, and finally the ultimate victories over sin and death on a tree made sacred by the most Holy Jesus.

As a Floridian surrounded by palm trees I dearly love, along with my new history lesson, I'll never look at Palm Sunday or palms the same way again.

ISABELLA CAMPOLATTARO

FAITH STEP

Research and contemplate images of these historical uses of the palm, then bring Jesus into the picture.

MONDAY
APRIL 14

Now upon the first day of the week, very early in the morning, they came unto the sepulchre, bringing the spices which they had prepared, and certain others with them.

LUKE 24:1 (KJV)

WITH MY HUSBAND FACING A daunting surgery we trust will eradicate his cancer, I've depended on praying friends to point us to the Healer. Sweetest are those who pray with confidence because they've seen Jesus work on their behalf in the past.

In preparation for celebrating the resurrection power of Jesus, I've been moved, too, by the faith of Jesus followers Mary and Martha, who, in keeping with Jewish tradition, would have likely helped prepare their brother Lazarus's body for burial. At the time of Jesus's death, the smell of spices might have still clung to their memories from their winding cloths around the body of their beloved sibling. Yes, the women watched their brother walk out of his tomb at

Jesus's command, resurrected from death. Certainly all three of them carried a powerful story of Jesus's miraculous ability to restore life "when the dead are gone."

I can't help but wonder if the sisters thought about Lazarus after Jesus was crucified. Could they have whispered to each other: "We saw Him raise our brother back to life. We watched it happen." Did their hearts dare anticipate that Jesus would miraculously rise again?

That's where my mind is resting regarding my husband and healing. Jesus has done it before. He can do it again. Are we approaching Resurrection Sunday—and anything that threatens us or those we love—with the same heartening thoughts?

CYNTHIA RUCHTI

FAITH STEP

Whether the need is provision, protection, or resurrection power, practice saying, "He's done it before. He can do it again" until hope rises.

TUESDAY
APRIL 15

*He went into all the country around
the Jordan, preaching a baptism of
repentance for the forgiveness of sins.*

LUKE 3:3 (NIV)

THE SANCTUARY WAS DIMLY LIT on that Easter Sunday as our pastor walked down the aisle. Chanting, he gently swung an incense lantern filling the room with mesmerizing scents.

The congregation held candles while our pastor led my son, Steven, and me down to the baptismal font. Steven and I held hands and exchanged solemn smiles.

As we took turns bending our heads over the font, the pastor dipped a seashell into the scented oil, pouring it over our heads. He anointed us three times with the sweet perfume, marking us as members on our journey with Christ.

Placing a white garment with gold stitching over our necks symbolized we had risen with Christ. Our baptismal candles were lit. Steven and I were now a part of the light.

St. Paul writes, "We were therefore buried with him through baptism into depth in order that, just as Christ was raised from the dead through the glory of the Father, we too may live a new life" (Romans 6:4, NIV).

Afterward, Steven and I walked back to our seats. We were still holding hands. Neither of us wanted to let go of the experience. Hopefully, we would remember the beautiful Easter service and never forget the meaning of our beautiful baptisms.

JEANNIE HUGHES

FAITH STEP

Write down three things you remember about your baptism. Pray on them and feel that special closeness to Jesus again.

WEDNESDAY
APRIL 16

God sees my ways and counts every step I take.

JOB 31:4 (NCV)

After my friend Pam and I go walking together, she tells me how many miles we covered—according to the step-counter app on her smartwatch. The other day, Mary announced at exercise class the number of steps she'd taken during our last workout together. Though I haven't jumped on the digital step-counter bandwagon yet, I'll happily claim the number of steps or accept the distance walked, even though I didn't personally count or take measurements.

But this only applies to *physical* exercise or walking. This doesn't apply to my faith walk. Just because someone I know or someone close to me practices a particular spiritual discipline or religious exercise, doesn't mean I can take credit for it. I can't claim the benefits of their spirituality or accept their faith walk as my own.

This made me wonder about the number of steps Jesus took to Golgotha. From information I found online, the distance Jesus walked to His crucifixion was approximately 650 yards, or just over one-third of a mile. Jesus anguished for about seven blocks, taking many slow, painful, difficult steps carrying a tree-sized cross. Meditating on this, I could sense Jesus whisper, "I walked those steps for *you*."

Because Jesus took those steps for me, I can claim the benefits that resulted from His walk to the cross: forgiveness for sin, salvation, new life in Him. And eternal life with Jesus in heaven when I've taken the last steps of my earthly walk in this life.

CASSANDRA TIERSMA

FAITH STEP

Take a prayer walk today—seven blocks,
if possible—thanking Jesus for those fateful steps
He took to the cross for you.

MAUNDY THURSDAY
APRIL 17

By this everyone will know that you are my disciples, if you love one another.

JOHN 13:35 (NIV)

WITH EACH PASSING YEAR, PEOPLE who know my mom often say I remind them more and more of her. I understand why they say it. I have a slender frame like she does, and we share a similar complexion. I've also been caught using many of the same gestures and facial expressions she has. Even my voice sounds a lot like hers—so much so that if we're on a phone call together, people have a hard time distinguishing which of us is talking.

In contrast, people who knew my late father say I look like him and his side of the family. If I were standing next to him, you would immediately notice I have his almond eyes, rounded nose, full lips, and heart-shaped face. I also inherited his athletic physique, specifically his naturally muscular arms. When I was younger, people wondered if I worked out regularly. I didn't. My arms appeared fit, but they were simply a reflection of my dad's genes.

What's true in the biological realm for me should also be true in the spiritual. As a follower of Jesus, I should embody all of His behaviors and traits. I should talk like Him. I should walk like Him. I should humble myself like Him. Most important, I should love like Him. Even if people don't know who Jesus is, when they see me, I should always be a reflection of Him.

ERICKA LOYNES

FAITH STEP

Write out John 13:35 and stick it to your mirror. Check it daily to make sure you're reflecting the image of Jesus.

GOOD FRIDAY
APRIL 18

I have told you all this so that you may have peace in me. Here on earth you will have many trials and sorrows. But take heart, because I have overcome the world.

JOHN 16:33 (NLT)

HAVE YOU EVER EXPERIENCED THE feeling that life as you know it was over? Maybe it was triggered by a dire medical diagnosis, financial ruin, or the breakup of a close relationship. Or a prodigal child's self-destructive choices, or the death of a loved one. Major life changes or losses can strike suddenly and make us feel like giving up. We wish we could lock ourselves behind closed doors, away from the world.

I can't imagine the disciples' feelings of confusion, shock, and loss when they saw Jesus arrested, tried, and sentenced to death. They'd given up everything to follow the man they assumed would deliver Israel from Rome (Luke 24:21). For 3 years they had witnessed Him heal diseases and perform miracles; they had been taught by Him. Now Jesus had been crucified and buried. They locked themselves in a house out of fear of the Jewish leaders (John 20:19). They didn't know that what seemed like a horrible ending would prove to be a wonderful beginning.

Our earthly suffering is temporary; it will lead us to a deeper relationship with Jesus or perhaps a new way to serve Him. But one day, life as we know it truly will be over. We'll step into a new beginning to spend eternity with Jesus in the perfect home He's prepared (John 14:3). Like Jesus's disciples, we'll discover that the glory of His presence obliterates the darkness of even our worst days.

DIANNE NEAL MATTHEWS

FAITH STEP

Are you grieving a loss or an ending? Memorize Jesus's words in John 16:33. Let His peace and hope wash over you.

HOLY SATURDAY
APRIL 19

*For in this hope we were saved. But hope that is seen
is no hope at all. Who hopes for what they already
have? But if we hope for what we do not yet have,
we wait for it patiently.*

ROMANS 8:24–25 (NIV)

O NE APRIL WEEKEND, MY FAMILY and I headed to the
Jersey Shore for our favorite amusement park's annual
half-price discount ticket sale. Once our summer season
passes were purchased, the kids went one way and my husband and I another. Meeting for one last ride before heading
home, we queued in line for Wild Waves. The popular roller
coaster's wait time was almost 45 minutes.

I wearily wished I was already asleep in bed. I argued with
myself about whether the ride was worth the extra time it
would take to arrive home. Meanwhile, my family chatted
happily with those around us, seemingly oblivious to waiting.

I admit, waiting is not easy for me. I tend to rush into
all the twists and turns of life instead of pausing for Jesus to

do His work. Sometimes I even take control, attempting to drive forward myself. But Jesus asks me to be patient and joyful while I wait on Him (Romans 12:12). So whether weary, frustrated, or anxious, I will do my level best to wait well on the ride of life. For Jesus is my ticket to happiness. No discount needed.

GLORIA JOYCE

FAITH STEP

Are you in a season of waiting? Whether it be test results or a vacation, ask Jesus to grant you patience while you wait.

EASTER SUNDAY
APRIL 20

"Come to me, all you who are weary and burdened, and I will give you rest. Take my yoke upon you and learn from me, for I am gentle and humble in heart, and you will find rest for your souls."

MATTHEW 11:28–29 (NIV)

"IF I WERE HOME TODAY, I would be in church. Many of you might be, as well," I said to the tour group I was leading. We were traveling on a motorcoach between Savannah and Jekyll Island, Georgia. "So, on this Easter Sunday, I'm going to take you to church."

The driver made a left turn onto a gravel lane and drove past a curious sign: Smallest Church in America, Deeded to Jesus Christ. A tiny cream-colored chapel with a white cross on top came into view.

"Agnes Harper, a local grocer, dreamed of a place where weary travelers could rest and think about Jesus. In 1949, she completed Christ's Chapel as a gift to the world. It measures only 10 feet by 15 feet, providing space for just twelve chairs and a podium. Inside, a beautiful stained-glass window features an image of Jesus ascending into the clouds."

We got off the motorcoach and guests snapped pictures. When they entered the chapel, I stood back and observed their responses. Some appeared interested in the history and culture of the site. Others seemed to do exactly what Agnes wished. They sat for a few moments, resting their bodies, focusing on the colorful depiction of the risen Christ. I too found refreshment in that small space as I pondered Jesus's immense gift to the world.

BECKY ALEXANDER

FAITH STEP

This Easter, seek the rest Jesus offers at church,
at home, or wherever you may roam.
Thank Him for His immense gift.

LENT & EASTER 2025
REFLECTIONS AND MEMORIES

LENT & EASTER 2025
REFLECTIONS AND MEMORIES

LENT & EASTER 2025
REFLECTIONS AND MEMORIES

LENT & EASTER 2025
REFLECTIONS AND MEMORIES

Contributors

Becky Alexander: page 34, 68, 96

Isabella Campolattaro: page 14, 56, 82

Pat Butler Dyson: page 4, 44, 74

Gwen Ford Faulkenberry: page 6, 48, 58

Heidi Gaul: page 22, 40, 76

Jeannie Hughes: page 16, 50, 86

Gloria Joyce: page 28, 64, 94

Jeanette Levellie: page 24, 42, 78

Ericka Loynes: page 30, 80, 90

Erin Keeley Marshall: page 18, 38, 72

Dianne Neal Matthews: page 8, 70, 92

Claire McGarry: page 32, 52, 66

Jennifer Anne F. Messing: page 10, 62

Cynthia Ruchti: page 26, 36, 84

Cassandra Tiersma: page 12, 54, 88

Kristen West: page 20, 46, 60

Acknowledgments

Scripture quotations marked (AMP) are taken from the *Amplified Bible*. Copyright © 2015 by The Lockman Foundation, La Habra, California. All rights reserved.

Scripture quotations marked (CEV) are taken from *Holy Bible: Contemporary English Version*. Copyright © 1995 American Bible Society.

Scripture quotations marked (KJV) are taken from the *King James Version of the Bible*.

Scripture quotations marked (MSG) are taken from *The Message*. Copyright © 1993, 2002, 2018 by Eugene H. Peterson.

Scripture quotations marked (NABRE) are taken from the *New American Bible,* revised edition, © 2010, 1991, 1986, 1970 Confraternity of Christian Doctrine, Inc., Washington, DC. All rights reserved.

Scripture quotations marked (NCV) are taken from *The Holy Bible, New Century Version*. Copyright © 2005 by Thomas Nelson.

Scripture quotations marked (NIV) are taken from *The Holy Bible, New International Version®, NIV®*. Copyright © 1973, 1978, 1984, 2011 by Biblica, Inc. Used by permission. All rights reserved worldwide.

Scripture quotations marked (NKJV) are taken from the *New King James Version®*. Copyright © 1982 by Thomas Nelson. Used by permission. All rights reserved.

Scripture quotations marked (NLT) are taken from the *Holy Bible, New Living Translation*. Copyright © 1996, 2004, 2007, 2015 by Tyndale House Foundation. Used by permission of Tyndale House Publishers Inc., Carol Stream, Illinois. All rights reserved.

Scripture quotations marked (TLB) are taken from *The Living Bible*. Copyright © 1971 by Tyndale House Publishers, Inc., Carol Stream, Illinois. All rights reserved.

A Note from the Editors

We hope you enjoyed *Walking with Jesus: Devotions for Lent & Easter 2025*, published by Guideposts. For over 75 years, Guideposts, a nonprofit organization, has been driven by a vision of a world filled with hope. We aspire to be the voice of a trusted friend, a friend who makes you feel more hopeful and connected.

By making a purchase from Guideposts, you join our community in touching millions of lives, inspiring them to believe that all things are possible through faith, hope, and prayer. Your continued support allows us to provide uplifting resources to those in need. Whether through our communities, websites, apps, or publications, we inspire our audiences, bring them together, and comfort, uplift, entertain, and guide them. Visit us at guideposts.org to learn more.

We would love to hear from you. Write us at Guideposts, P.O. Box 5815, Harlan, Iowa 51593 or call us at (800) 932-2145. Did you love *Walking with Jesus: Devotions for Lent & Easter 2025*? Leave a review for this product on guideposts.org/shop. Your feedback helps others in our community find relevant products.

Find inspiration, find faith, find Guideposts.

Shop our best sellers and favorites at
guideposts.org/shop

Or scan the QR code to go directly to our Shop